Insects

Joy Richardson

W

FRANKLIN WATTS

LONDON•SYDNEY

This edition 2003

Franklin Watts
96 Leonard Street
London EC2A 4XD

Franklin Watts Australia
45-51 Huntley Street
Alexandria
NSW 2015

Editors: Sarah Ridley and Sally Luck
Designer: Janet Watson
Illustrator: Linda Costello
Picture Researcher: Sarah Moule

Photographs: Bruce Coleman Ltd 7, 9, 14, 16, 21;
Robert Harding Picture Library 19; Frank Lane
Picture Agency 13; Natural History
Photographic Agency cover; 10, 22, 25, 27

A CIP catalogue record for this book is available from the British Library

ISBN: 0 7496 5313 2

Printed in Malaysia

Contents

The world is full of insects.

For every single person in the world there
are about a hundred million insects.
There are hundreds of thousands of
different types of insect.

Good and bad

The world needs insects. They can
do a lot of damage but they do a
lot of good work, too.

▶ Insects are everywhere in our world.

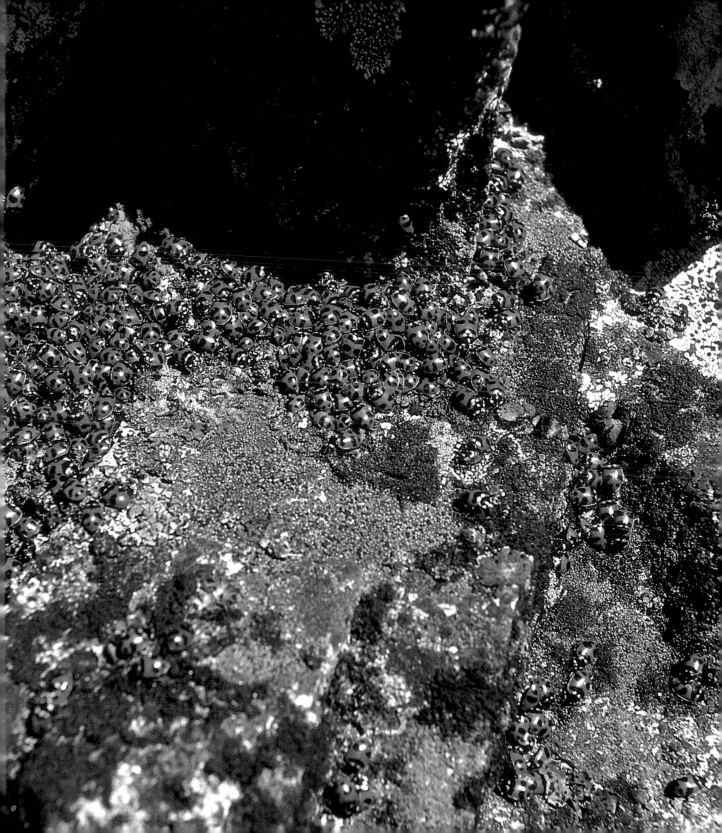

Laying eggs

All insects start life inside an egg.

Female insects lay eggs through tubes
at the back of their body.

Where do insects lay eggs?
Some insects drill into leaves or seeds
to lay their eggs. Some lay their eggs
in holes underground. Some glue their
eggs in place with a sticky liquid
that their bodies make.

▶ This butterfly is laying her eggs. She is
gluing them to the underside of a leaf.

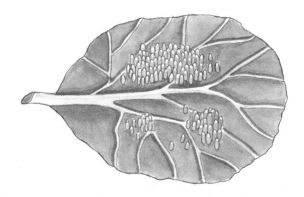

Starting life

A newborn insect is called a **larva**. Most insect larvae are nothing like their parents.

Caterpillars

When a butterfly egg **hatches**, a caterpillar crawls out. The caterpillar feeds on plants. It **sheds** its skin several times as it grows longer and fatter.

When it is fully grown, the caterpillar prepares for a big change.

◄ These caterpillars look very different from the butterflies they will become.

All change

When a caterpillar is ready to become an adult, it stops feeding.

It fixes itself to a plant and spins a **cocoon** around its body. The cocoon protects the caterpillar, which is now called a **pupa**.

The pupa stays very still inside its case while its whole body changes and its legs and **wings** start to grow.

A new butterfly
Some pupae stay inside their case for just a few days, but some will stay inside for over a year. When the caterpillar has finished changing into a butterfly, it breaks out of its cocoon.

▶ This monarch butterfly has just broken out of its cocoon.

Growing up

Different insects grow up
in different ways.

Bees and wasps make **nests**. The larvae live
safely in the nest until they change into adults.

Stick insects hatch from their egg looking like
tiny adults. As they grow bigger, they shed
old skin and replace it with new skin.

Caddis fly larvae live underwater. They make
cases of stones and shells to hide in while they
grow their wings.

◀ A caddis fly larva emerges
from the case it has made.

A skeleton on the outside

An insect has no bones. Its **skeleton** is on the outside of its body.

The cuticle
An insect's skeleton is a case of tough skin called the **cuticle**. All the muscles which move the legs and wings are attached to the inside of the cuticle.

Protection
The cuticle protects the insect's soft insides and helps to stop them drying out.

◀ This male stag beetle has a tough cuticle, which helps to prevent other animals eating it.

A body in three parts

Adult insects have three parts to their body.

The three parts
The head is at the front of the body.
The **thorax** is in the middle and has the legs and wings attached to it.
The **abdomen** is at the back. It is usually the biggest part.

A body in segments
Each part is made up of **segments**.
This helps the body to bend.

▶ This photograph clearly shows the three body parts of a wasp: the head, the thorax and the large abdomen.

Breathing

Insects do not breathe through their mouths.

Air holes

They take in air through **air holes** along the sides of their body. Tubes from the air holes branch out to every part of the body.

Oxygen for energy

Oxygen from the air passes into the muscles to make energy. Lots of air goes to the thorax where energy is needed to drive the legs and wings.

▶ This death's head hawkmoth caterpillar has nine air holes along each side of its body.

Legs

All insects have six legs attached to the thorax.

The legs bend at the joints where the cuticle is very thin.

Walking steadily

Insects are steady walkers. They keep a triangle of three legs on the ground while they move the other three.

Walking upside down

On the ends of their legs there are tiny claws and sticky pads. These help with walking upside down.

◄ Crane flies can hang themselves from plants by using the claws and sticky pads at the ends of their feet.

Wings

Most insects can fly. They have one or two pairs of wings attached to the thorax.

Muscles make the wings move. Some flies can beat their wings hundreds of times in a second.

Beetles
Beetles hide their wings away. When they fly, the front covers lift and the back wings unfold.

Dragonflies
Dragonflies keep their wings spread out to glide and swoop on smaller insects.

▶ The emperor dragonfly has huge wings and can fly very quickly.

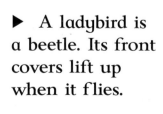

▶ A ladybird is a beetle. Its front covers lift up when it flies.

Heads

An insect has two large eyes and two **antennae** on its head.

Eyes
An insect's eyes are on the sides of its head which means that it can see all around. Insects cannot see very clearly but they can spot the smallest movements.

Antennae
Insects have antennae on the front of their head. Antennae collect information about touch, taste, sounds and smells.

▶ This photograph clearly shows the large eyes and antennae of a moth.

Insect facts

All insects lay eggs. They have skeletons on the outside and their bodies have three parts made up of segments. They have air holes along their sides and have six legs attached to the thorax. All insects have large eyes and antennae on their heads.

Not insects

Not all creepy crawly creatures are insects, though they may have a lot in common. Worms, woodlice, centipedes and spiders are not insects.

Glossary

abdomen The large, back-most part of an insect's body.

air holes Insects breathe by taking in air through air holes along the sides of their bodics.

antennae Long, thin body parts attached to the front of an insect's head. Antennae help the insect to touch, taste, hear and smell.

cocoon The silk case spun by a caterpillar to protect it while it changes into a butterfly.

cuticle The tough skin on the outside of an insect which forms its skeleton.

hatch To break out of an egg.

larva (larvae) The name given to an insect, and some other animals, before they are fully grown.

nest Some insects and other animals build nests to lay their eggs in and to house their babies.

oxygen The substance that all living things need in order to breathe and stay alive.

pupa (pupae) While a caterpillar is turning into a butterfly, it is called a pupa.

segments Each part of an insect's body is made up of small sections called segments.

shed When the top layer of an animal's skin comes off.

skeleton The framework of an animal to which muscles are attached. An insect's skeleton is on the outside of its body.

thorax The middle part of an insect's body, to which the legs and wings are attached.

wing The part of an insect's body that is used for flying. Insects have one or two pairs of wings.

Index